THE DECOUPAGE BOOK

Decoupage sphere, by Tom Sullivan

The Decoupage Book

More Than 60 Decorative Projects Using Simple Techniques

Holly Boswell

A Sterling/Lark Book
Sterling Publishing Co., Inc. New York

Design: Dana Irwin
Production: Elaine Thompson, Dana Irwin
Photography: Evan Bracken

Boswell, Holly.
    The decoupage book : more than 60 decorative projects
using simple techniques / Holly Boswell.
        p.   cm.
    "A Sterling/Lark book."
    Includes index.
    ISBN 0-8069-0610-3
    1. Decoupage.   I. Title.
TT870.B654   1993
745.54'6--dc20   93-36461
                                                 CIP

10 9 8 7 6 5 4

A Sterling/Lark Book

First paperback edition published in 1995 by
Sterling Publishing Company, Inc.
387 Park Avenue South, New York, N.Y. 10016

Produced by Altamont Press, Inc.
50 College Street, Asheville, NC 28801

© 1994 by Altamont Press

Distributed in Canada by Sterling Publishing
    ℅ Canadian Manda Group, One Atlantic Avenue, Suite 105
    Toronto, Ontario, Canada M6K 3E7
Distributed in Great Britain and Europe by Cassell PLC
    Villiers House, 41/47 Strand, London WC2N 5JE, England
Distributed in Australia by Capricorn Link (Australia) Pty Ltd.
    P.O. Box 6651, Baulkham Hills, Business Centre, NSW 2153, Australia

Sterling ISBN 0-8069-0610-3 Trade
            0-8069-0611-1 Paper

Contents

Introduction and History **6**

Traditional Decoupage Process

Design Considerations **12**
  Selecting the foundation
  Sources of decorative materials

Preparing the Foundation **18**
  Wood in various conditions
  Metals
  Ceramics, glass, plaster and stone
  Gesso techniques

Applying Decorative Papers **22**
  Preparing a print
  Methods of coloring
  Cutting techniques
  Pasting and burnishing

Techniques for Finishing **26**
  Considering the options
  Traditional varnishing
  Sanding and waxing
  Avoiding common flaws

Variations and New Techniques **30**
  Traditional Variations
  New Foundations
  New Decorative Materials
  New Finishing Techniques

Projects

Elementary Decoupage **34**
Collage Decoupage **44**
Traditional Decoupage **62**
Elevated Decoupage **80**
Repoussé **88**
Potichomania **94**
Eggshell Decoupage **105**

Decoupage Prints **110**

Glossary **127**

Credits **128**

Index **128**

Introduction and History

The term "decoupage" comes from the French *découper*—to cut out. It has come to refer to the decorative art of applying paper cutouts to a surface. The origins of this craft are apparently diverse, having been a folk art that grew in sophistication and eventually found its way into the royal courts of Europe. Yet the true marvel of decoupage remains how such striking and exquisite effects can be achieved by such simple means.

This is a craft for anyone. The skills are easily mastered, and the materials involve minimal expense. In fact, the components are often recycled from salvage. You can invest as much or as little time as you like, and you can create pleasing results at any level of workmanship. Of course, the more beautifully designed and painstakingly executed a piece is, the more it will be valued and appreciated as a real work of art.

The popular practice of decoupage has evolved through many

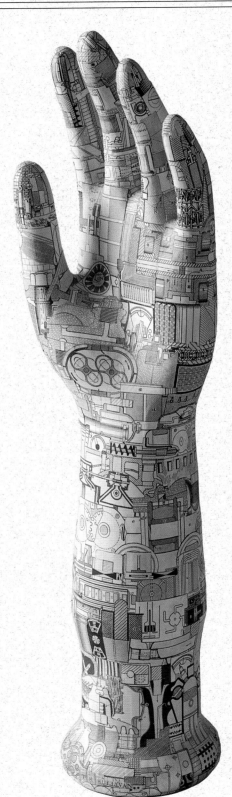

Porcelain hand with decoupage of textbook illustrations, by Tom Sullivan

Ironing board, iron and hangers with decoupage
of 1960s dress patterns,
by Ellen Zahorec 7

periods of resurgence. The last minor eruption, occurring in the sixties with trendy pop art pasted on plaques and other tacky knick-knacks, was a fad most decoupeurs are anxious to forget. In the whole of Western culture, however, there are three major classifications of decoupage: 18th Century, Victorian and Contemporary.

Decoupage in the 18th century, now regarded as "classic" or "traditional" decoupage, consisted primarily of hand-colored prints of the day cut out and pasted onto furniture or other furnishings and buried under many coats of finish. This resulted from early efforts in Italy, known as *arte povero* (poor man's art), to copy and compete with the fine lacquer work being imported from China and Japan. This style and technique was soon replicated throughout Europe, but most successfully in England, where it was called *japanning.* French decoupage distinguished itself with very intricate cutting of delicate motifs,

dainty flowers, cherubs and the like. Various other styles were developed in Portugal, Poland, Belgium and else-where.

Popular 18th century engravings by such artists as Francoise Boucher, Jean-Baptiste Pillement, Jean-Antoine Watteau, Thomas Bewick and Martin Englebrecht were most prominently used in decoupage of this period. Many of these engravings were collected into a single volume by Robert Sayer and sold to decoupeurs as *The Ladies' Amusement Book*. This was during a time when families and their guests would entertain them-selves by cutting out designs for decoupage together. Noble people like Marie Antoinette and Lord Byron were among those who enjoyed the artful diversion of decoupage.

Victorian decoupage was more three-dimensional, incorpo-rating embossed, precolored images from die-cut scrap-books, along with gold paper braid, into

highly ornate designs. These embossed cutouts were used in Germany to decorate Biedermeier furniture.

Contemporary decoupage utilizes the vast array of printed matter available today as well as new glues, sealants and finishes. Thicker papers and other materials are not inappropriate, since traditional gluing and styles of finishing are no longer a constraint. Now that these parameters have been opened up, decoupage is free to explore the realms of montage and collage. Designs which overlap or reach out into bold relief are now valid and acceptable. Images and shapes found on non-paper materials are now worthy and useable. The potential for decoupage into the 21st century is wide open.

Reading this book will equip you with a working knowledge of basic techniques, as well as an exciting glimpse into the future of decoupage. There will always be newer and more wonderful ways to cut out and apply designs to decorate a surface. The newest discoveries are waiting for you.

10

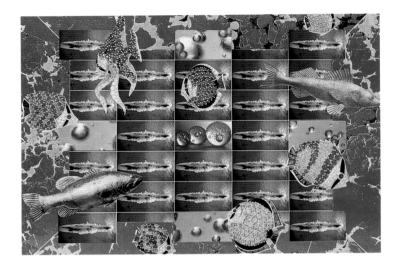

Three Collages by Terry Taylor

Collage by Ellen Zahorec

Traditional Decoupage Process

Design Considerations

It doesn't matter whether you choose your foundation and collect decorative material independently, together, or one long before the other. The goal is always a marriage of the two. Good composition and design sense are largely intuitive. Interesting effects can be achieved by following basic rules of design, but also by deciding when to defy those rules. Ultimately, it's a matter of personal taste.

Play with your design before committing it to scissors and paste. Let new and unexpected things happen. Try different combinations of design elements: colors, shapes, textures, sizes and positions. Consider altering the background. Decide if you want to create a focal point, use a repeating motif, or how best to enhance a particular feature of your foundation. This is the most creative phase of any project, and deserves to be played out fully so that it is worthy of the time you will invest executing it.

Selecting the foundation

With proper surface preparation, there is almost no limit to the objects that can be decorated with decoupage. Transforming an ordinary object into a work of art is perhaps the most gratifying aspect of this highly versatile craft. Adventurous decoupeurs will even create their own objects and surfaces out of wood, ceramics, paper-mâché and other materials. Beginners, however, should attempt smaller, simpler projects before getting involved with more intricate, time-consuming ones.

Traditional decoupage of Boucher cherubs and scrolls, by Polly Degas

These are some of the most common foundations suitable for decoupage:

all kinds of boxes and trays, plates, bowls, cups and vases, picture frames, plaques and mirrors, lamps, shades and sconces, book covers and book ends, all kinds of tables, chairs, cabinets, chests, bureaus, desks, bed headboards, boudoir accessories, waste baskets, light switch plates, wall panels, screens, valances, cornices, mantelpieces, pianos...

Decoupage mirror, by Cynthia Alderdice

Oriental decoupage box,
by Happy Veirs

Oriental decoupage with mother-of-pearl,
by Happy Veirs

14

Potichomania on vase, by Ann Douglas

15

Sources of decorative materials

Decoupage in the 18th century relied heavily upon lithographs by popular artists of the day. Nowadays we are able to take advantage of a wonderful array of printed media. Still, it pays to select designs which have artistic value, are deserving of current interests, and printed with fine inks on quality papers. Magazines and newspapers will bleed, fade and disintegrate. However, images can be reproduced in black & white or color using a photocopier. Use the thinner paper stocks for traditional decoupage.

Sources of interesting materials can be found in all sorts of places, especially if you remain vigilant. Browse at book shops—both new and old—antique stores and auctions, flea markets and garage sales, thrift stores…even your own attic. You can find newer materials at stationery and gift shops, print shops, museum gift shops, five-and-dimes and department stores.

Here are some items to look for:

engravings, lithographs, etchings, block prints, facsimile editions of engravings & woodcuts, illustrations in children's books, old art books, art prints, portfolios, calendars, posters, wallpaper, gift wrapping paper, foil backed with paper, maps, old documents, coats of arms, stationery, post cards, greeting cards, old or foreign money, unusual postage stamps, catalogs, even junk mail...

Decoupage requires minimal tools and materials.

Preparing the Foundation

A foundation may be made of various substances: wood, metal, ceramic and glass are the most prevalent. What is important about a properly prepared surface is that it be structurally sound, smooth, clean, sealed, and colored appropriately for your design. Then again, you may want to cover your foundation entirely with papers or other sheeting. Wallpaper paste works well for large areas. Wrinkles should be pressed out with a rolling pin. A small roller (brayer) can be used for smaller surfaces.

Wood in various conditions

If the foundation object has loose seams or is otherwise unsturdy, repair it with a good carpenter's glue. Clamp with vises or by wrapping with strips of old rubber inner tubes while drying to achieve tight seams. Dents, nail holes and other imperfections can be filled with any number of commercial wood fillers, then sanded with wet/dry sandpapers.

Raw wood should be sanded, with the grain, using #100 garnet paper, followed by #220. Sand thoroughly around lid seams for a loose fit before applying sealer and paint—especially if the seams were previously painted. After sanding, rub with a tack cloth before staining or sealing. The rule is: stain before you seal, and seal before you paint.

Water-soluble alcohol-base stains or water-diluted acrylics are recommended. Wipe off excess with a rag, and allow the stain to dry thoroughly. Water-base stains can be sealed with two coats of one part shellac with one part denatured alcohol, or an acrylic emulsion (polymer medium). *Always read the labels of whatever product you are using.*

Shellac is the sealant of choice, but should never be used over any other finish—only raw wood. It can also be used (in two coats) before applying oil-base paints, after one hour of drying. Shellac can get gummy after six months' of storage. Store it in tightly sealed glass containers to prevent darkening. It should be stirred before use—never shaken, which makes it bubbly. Apply it in a dry environment, since moisture makes it "bloom" (get milky). If this happens, apply denatured alcohol and let dry.

To apply shellac to raw wood, load the brush, then press out the excess against the inside of the container, to prevent bubbling. Begin at the center of a surface and stroke quickly outward to the edge, then back to the center and out to the opposite edge. Reduce the brush load for contoured areas. Touch up gaps or excess by tapping the end bristles of the brush into these areas. If the brush hardens, restore it with alcohol or one part ammonia with one part water—never soap. For quick and easy projects, consider using an acrylic spray sealer.

Wood that has been previously varnished can be rubbed clean with denatured alcohol. Sanding with #100 garnet paper will further prepare the surface. Wood that has been well painted should be treated in the reverse: sanded and then rubbed with alcohol (or mineral spirits or turpentine for old wax or grease). If you are refinishing a piece of furniture that has been sprayed with anything containing silicone, there may be little you can do to reapply varnish effectively. Wood that has deteriorating paint may need filling, sanding, sealing raw areas with shellac, or even scraping and stripping with heavy-duty paint removers. An alcohol rub and sanding will complete the process.

If you choose to paint your foundation, check the compatibility of your paint with the base sealant. Oil versus water is the primary choice. Flat enamels or latex acrylics are preferable. Use an appropriate sealer over metallic paints where the decoupage is to be pasted, or else the metallic powder will compromise the paste. A final decoupage finish of varnish will adhere to flat enamel best, as will water-base polyurethane to flat latex paints.

Apply the paint evenly with a brush, thinly and frugally, to achieve a smooth surface. Thin the paint if it's lumpy or thickened, use less, and let dry thoroughly between coats.

Metals

Preparing metal is actually easier than wood, but different materials are required, and rust is a big factor. After sanding rust, you can use a magnet, a vacuum cleaner, and a tack rag to clean the surface. Apply metal primer and let it dry overnight.

Old metal that has been painted and is damaged can be cleaned with paint or rust remover using a brush or scraper. Hammer out any dents, sand and wash with alcohol before priming. Old metal that is unpainted might require rust remover, sandpaper or steel wool, then an alcohol rub.

New metal that is galvanized should be washed with vinegar or a diluted acetic acid (to be used with caution). Sand lightly if necessary to create a smooth surface. No primer will be required. If the metal is not galvanized, sand and wash it with alcohol before priming it. If new metal has been painted, remove the old gloss with fine sandpaper for good adhesion. Use rust-inhibiting paints if possible.

Ceramics, glass, plaster and stone

This alternative list of materials could also include glossy metals and leather. In general, to prepare these surfaces, pre-clean with soap and water, then wipe with denatured alcohol. Acrylic or mat urethane sealer should be sprayed in 2-3 light coats, then allowed to dry thoroughly.

For plaster, stone and leather, you should apply 3-4 thin coats of shellac an hour apart instead of spray sealer. Unglazed ceramics require two generous coats.

Gesso techniques

Water-base acrylic gesso is versatile and easy to use. A thin base coat will seal the grain of raw wood. One or two successive coats will cover minor surface flaws. For ceramics and metal, two coats are sufficient. One coat over a sealer can be used on glass.

Watercolors (in tubes) can be mixed directly with gesso for tinting. Never mix gesso with oil-base paints, and keep your water-base and oil-base brushes separate. Stir well and apply the gesso with a stiff-bristle water-dampened brush, fully loaded. Use quick, light strokes in different directions. After it dries, sand with #400 wet/dry sandpaper (moistened) in a circular motion. For a high sheen, polish with dampened china silk wrapped around your fingers.

Acrylic paints can be applied directly to this gesso base. For oil-base paints, prime the gesso with alcohol-diluted shellac. Spray paints can be used, but watch for base compatibility.

To restore old gesso, chip off loose areas and sand down to the foundation. A vinyl filler may be needed to rebuild these areas. Re-seal with shellac.

Going to Market

The Angler

CUNNINGHAM ART PRODUCTS

© B. P. CO.

53316

Old prints for traditional decoupage
can be found in many places.

Applying Decorative Papers

Traditional decoupage uses paper—usually thin paper—as opposed to fabric or other materials. Most often, if color needs to be added, oil pencils are used. Still, there are many possibilities, and artful cutting is the key.

Preparing a print

Watch for inks that bleed, such as alcohol-soluble or aniline dyes in liquid-ready watercolors, certain magazines, greeting cards or calendars. Test this by applying your alcohol-soluble sealer to a sample area. If it bleeds, try an acrylic spray. Also test your varnish. If the inks bleed after application, they're not useable. If your print has another image printed on the back, spray both sides with clear acrylic sealer. If there is still show-through, paint the back with white acrylic paint.

Prints on thick paper should be thinned for traditional decoupage, or else labor-intensive varnishing will be necessary to achieve a smooth finish. One method of thinning involves moistening the back of the print with white vinegar for a few minutes. Excess paper can then be rubbed off with a damp sponge. Rinse off the vinegar, let dry, then spray with sealer. Another method would be to spray the printed side with three coats of clear acrylic sealer. Once dry, excess paper can be peeled from the back after soaking five minutes in warm water

Methods of coloring

Oil pencils are preferred over watercolor pencils because of their richer colors, but either can be used the same way. Areas of your print can be filled in an even, cartoon-like fashion, or contoured with shadows and highlights for a three-dimensional effect.

To recreate 18th century color schemes, shade lightly with terra-cotta, or use grayish tones throughout. When contouring, begin with lighter shades and progress into darker ones. Different colors can be added for effective shading and highlighting. Objects depicted in the foreground should be colored more vividly, with muted tones and pastels toward the background. Keep your pencils sharpened.

Watercolors can be brushed on quite nicely. Compared to pencils, their application is faster, their colors more intense, and they have a style all their own. Avoid colors that are opaque. Acrylics thinned with water can create the same effect as watercolor, but cannot be sponged or blended once they dry.

It is important to seal the print after you have colored it. This prevents smearing during the gluing and varnishing processes. It also strengthens the paper prior to cutting, although some papers are already too stiff and must be sealed after cutting. Three parts shellac mixed with one part alcohol can be brushed on to seal the print. Clear acrylic sealer with a mat finish is sometimes preferable. Spray two light coats, three minutes apart, on each side.

Cutting techniques

This is the very heart of decoupage. Skillful cutting and effective cutting patterns are crucial to the enjoyment and artistry of the craft. Cuticle scissors are the primary tool for curved and intricate cuts. Embroidery scissors will handle the straight and longer cuts. An X-acto knife may be preferred for certain cuts, but is not a traditional tool.

Scissors should be held with the thumb and middle finger, with the blades supported by the index finger. This hand simply works the scissors and remains stationary while the other hand feeds the paper into the base of the blades at constantly shifting angles. The tips of the blades are only used for cutting into tight spaces. The curve of the cuticle scissors should be angled away from the print. Practice all kinds of cuts on scrap material before attempting your first project.

The general procedure is to first cut away all the excess paper around your design for easier handling. Then cut away any inside areas. When cutting out tiny openings, stab a hole from the top, then cut out the shape from underneath. The outer edge is cut out last. Whenever there are delicate, extended portions of a pattern, you should draw and cut connecting "ladders." These bridges will hold the pattern together while you're cutting and also while applying glue, and can be cut away just before pasting the image down. If you are cutting a large pattern, or accidentally cut your design apart, manageable sections can be rejoined in the gluing process.

All of your cutting should enhance the character and features of the design—not simply follow the outlines. This is a hallmark of fine decoupage. There are many approaches to cutting, each dependent upon and inspired by the shapes of the design. Serrated edges adhere and often look better than straight ones. Fine-line and feathery outlines create elegant silhouettes. Foreground and background contours can be designated within both positive and negative spaces. For repeating motifs, pin two together and cut them as one. But most importantly, you should explore your own imagination.

Pasting and burnishing

Water-soluble decoupage paste (sold as such) is most suitable for lighter weight papers and delicately cut designs. Standard white glues (PVA or PVC) that are thinned to three parts with one part water will work for heavier papers. This proportion can be adjusted as necessary. Glue should be stored in a small, wide-mouth container

and stirred frequently during use. Adhesium (a paint and wallpaper supply) can be used to prime slick foundations like glass, metal and lacquered surfaces before a print is pasted down. As always, read all labels.

First, assemble the following items: paste or glue, a bowl of water, tweezers, a sponge, a clean cloth or paper towels, waxed paper, a small roller (brayer) or spoon, or a stainless steel burnishing tool (optional). Prepare a clean work space, covered with newspapers.

It is prudent to position your designs on the foundation and mark a few corners or key areas lightly with a pencil before applying paste. Then lay each design face down on waxed paper and apply paste or glue thinly and evenly with a brush, sponge, or—best of all—your fingers. Cover completely, or else uncovered areas will bubble up when varnish is later applied. Wash and dry your fingers frequently throughout the process.

Place each design section onto the foundation one at a time. Tweezers are most useful for small areas. Tap them down into place with a slightly moistened sponge, gently squeezing out any excess glue, and wiping it up. Cover the design with waxed paper and roll it out with a brayer, always from the center. Remove the waxed paper and sponge away any glue, then blot and wipe with a dry cloth or paper towels. If your design is large, you may need to repeat this process.

After 24 hours of drying, wipe away excess glue with a damp sponge or cloth. Very stubborn spots can be removed with vinegar, but stay away from the design. The acid in vinegar can discolor your print. If your design paper is thick, you can bevel the edges with a burnisher. The spoon-shaped end is for flat areas, while the pointed end works well on narrow crevices and angles. A clear acrylic spray is optional at this stage.

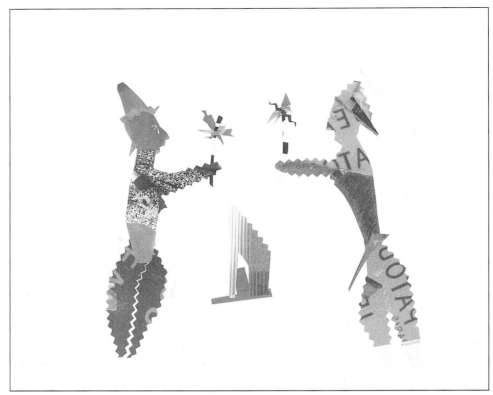

"Conflict Resolution" collage, by Brigid Burns

Untitled collage, by Brigid Burns

A Nuestra Madre de las Americas

"A Nuestra Madre de las Americas" collage,   by Brigid Burns

Techniques for Finishing

Traditional decoupage finish does more than protect the finished piece. The lavish application of many coats creates a special feel and style that is uniquely decoupage. Nonetheless, there are different ways of achieving pleasing results.

Considering the options

Varnish has long been the most favored finish, although shellac was used when the craft first emerged. Varnish can be thinned with turpentine and cleaned up with paint remover. You must allow 24 hours between coats, and 10-20 is an average number of coats. There are many varnishes available commercially. Their properties vary, so read their labels. A traditional shortcut is lacquer, or one of its derivatives. It is both thinned and cleaned up with lacquer thinner, and requires only four hours between coats. However, lacquer cannot be used over oil paints or flat enamels. There are other contemporary water-base options which will be discussed in the next section.

Traditional varnishing

When varnishing over oil paint or flat enamel, check the label to make sure the varnish doesn't need to be cleaned up with lacquer thinner. If so, this kind of varnish will shrivel the paint. Test a sample before you begin if you're in doubt. When varnishing over water-base paint, make sure the paint has fully cured. Flaws can show up even years later. If you want an antique effect, use a mild amber varnish, but keep in mind that most all varnishes will yellow within a few years. Never mix different kinds or brands of varnish.

Always work in a clean, dust-free, well-lit area with minimal humidity. Stir the varnish gently before each application. Dip your brush about halfway into the varnish, then touch it to the side of the container to drain the excess. Start at the center with smooth,

even strokes, each one in the opposite direction from before. Apply lightly at the edges to avoid build-up. Brush away drips or particles as you go. Dust with a tack rag before each new coat.

Depending on the thickness of your decoupage and intended style, up to 10 coats should be applied before the first sanding. Up to 10 more coats should be applied before the final two coats of a low gloss varnish, which is then rubbed with steel wool before waxing. Any paper lining, such as inside a box, should be sprayed with a sealer, then coated twice with varnish.

Brushes can be stored in turpentine between daily applications. A glass baby bottle with the nipple tip snipped off will hold and seal the handle. Always use a glass container. Varnish cannot be stored for long periods.

Sanding and waxing

As noted above, sanding is an intermediate step in the varnishing process to remove high spots. Wait two full days before wet-sanding, and use #400 wet/dry sandpaper. Remove the milky residue with a wet sponge, then a tack rag. Sand lightly so as not to expose any elements of your piece. Between the second varnishing and the final low gloss finish, follow sandpapering with #0000 steel wool, then the tack rag.

Steel wool refines the work of sandpaper and is used in a circular motion. Surfaces must always be dry before using steel wool. If you wish to smooth a contour rather than a flat area, use steel wool. Allow a month before the final waxing so the varnish can cure fully.

Waxing covers minute scratches caused by the sanding process, and bestows a marvelous patina and feel to the work. Use a decoupage wax, varnish wax or fine furniture wax. Rub it firmly on with a slightly damp cloth in a circular motion. Buff with a soft dry cloth, and you are done. If you ever have to repair a piece, first remove all the wax with fine sandpaper and steel wool.

Avoiding common flaws

Varnish lumps can form in the storage container or get trapped in the bristles of a brush, then show up during application. Keep containers tightly sealed. Lumps can be skimmed out with a spoon or strained through old pantyhose. A dried lump can be sanded off with #400 wet/dry sandpaper.

Varnish drips must be avoided in both the application and sanding phases. Work in a well-lit area. Don't load your brush too heavily. Brush away drips as they occur, especially around edges. Once dry, they should be sanded off with #400 wet/dry sandpaper before applying the next coat.

Dirt or dust may contaminate wet varnish as it is being applied. Wipe any particles away with a cloth as soon as you notice them. If a large area is contaminated, gently remove all the wet varnish with a cloth dipped in distilled alcohol, then let dry thoroughly before the next coat. Flaws which have already dried will have to be sanded off with #400 wet/dry sandpaper.

Bubbles can form on the paper, usually after many coats of varnish and even several weeks after the piece has been finished. Using an appropriate glue and applying it thoroughly to the decoupage will minimize this problem. If a bubble appears, cut a slit at the edge with a razor blade, insert glue with a toothpick, then press it gently back down. Wipe away excess glue, let dry and refinish.

Poorly glued edges may pop up during varnishing. If the varnish is still wet, remove it with a cloth dipped in distilled alcohol. Lift up the edge and reapply glue with a toothpick, then press it back down and let it dry thoroughly. Sometimes edges curl up slightly, even after the varnish is dry. Sand them lightly and apply a few more coats of varnish.

Bloom refers to the cloudiness in a supposedly dry coat of varnish which can occur in excessive humidity. This can be prevented by working in a dry space and allowing adequate drying time between coats. Bloom will usually disappear with the application of the next coat. If not, wipe the dried surface gently with a cloth dipped in distilled alcohol, and allow more drying time between coats.

Cracks can open up in varnish or lacquer over time, or during application if the undercoat wasn't fully dry. Cracks in an old piece can be filled in by removing all the old wax and refinishing it. If cracking occurs during application, allow extra drying time before subsequent coats of varnish. Applying more than a half dozen coats of lacquer will often result in cracking, so stop at that point.

Raw paper can be exposed if you rub too vigorously or too soon in the varnishing process. Touch up the image with colored pencils or ink where necessary, let dry, then continue with coats of varnish.

Mixed media decoupage on fans, by Happy Veirs

Oshié decoupage, by Carol Perry

Oshié decoupage, by Carol Perry

Oshié decoupage, by Carol Perry

Variations and New Techniques

Ever since the beginnings of this highly versatile craft, there has been a progression of natural variations and departures. New approaches and techniques will continue as materials, technologies, experience and imagination evolve. In this way, the craft of decoupage can remain viable as an art form.

This chapter will survey many early variations before exploring some new approaches to the three fundamental parameters of decoupage: foundations, decorative materials and ways of finishing. Many of these new techniques will be explained more fully in the various instructions for projects which follow.

Traditional Variations

The **Creil** technique originated in 18th century England and was copied extensively in France. The method involved transferring images from an engraved copper plate directly onto white porcelain. This process was eventually replaced with a method involving gelatin transfers. A classic border motif always surrounded the central design. Black images on a white background were most common, although yellow was sometimes used for borders or as the background.

Toleware is made of tin and was used as an inexpensive substitute for porcelain. It was painted yellow before designs of black were painted on in order to imitate the creil effect. When prints were cut out they were usually left black on white, then pasted over the yellow foundation, creating a very distinctive style.

Marquetry is a form of inlay where different shades of wood veneer are cut out and arranged in patterns. This can be simulated in decoupage using faux wood papers.

Boulle is another variation of inlay that utilizes tortoise shell inlaid with brass scrolls. Faux tortoise shell and gold tea chest papers can be substituted in the decoupage process. Similar inlay effects can be achieved with marbleized papers, known as **intarsia**, or other decorative papers.

Trompe l'oeil has long been a favorite style of decoupeurs. The goal of this technique is to fool the eye into seeing a flat surface as three-dimensional. The use of perspective and shadows (often hand-painted) are crucial to the illusion.

Potichomania caught on in 19th century England. Cutout prints were pasted inside a clear glass vase, then painted inside to create the effect of fine porcelain. The glass acts as both foundation and protective finish, saving the tedium of varnishing. The original intent was to recreate Greek and Etruscan vases by simulating rare and expensive Sevrés porcelain.

Repoussé, sometimes called **moulage**, involves embossing images on heavy paper, usually filling the cavities with supporting material, and finishing the relief as decoupage. Often, areas of high relief are cut out, molded, filled and reattached to a background which is either flat or partially embossed into shallow relief.

New Foundations

With today's improved selection of primers, sealants and adhesives, it is possible to decorate virtually any solid object with decoupage. There is greater opportunity than ever before to do imaginative treatments on household items like kitchen appliances, lunch boxes, televisions, toys, luggage, and all sorts of furnishings. You can even go outside and decorate your mailbox, porch furniture, bicycles and other vehicles, or equipment around the workplace. Decoupage is a craft with few boundaries.

Glass provides a versatile foundation for designs, either under or over the surface. Glass-topped tables, mirrors, windows, lamps, plates, bowls, vases and jars are a good beginning. When affixing decoupage under glass, the background colorant can be either opaque or transluscent for effective backlighting.

Acrylics and plastics are also quite useable as foundations. Plastics need only to be cleaned with alcohol, and should usually not be painted. Use a commercial "spray mount" or rubber cement when applying decoupage cutout materials.

Woods, metals, ceramics, plaster and stone were discussed in the chapter on traditional process as suitable foundation materials. Add to this list other materials such as leather, cork, styrofoam and paper-mâché. These can be sculpted into any shape you desire as a foundation. Paper-mâché is a wonderfully versatile material. It can be fashioned using a variety of methods, and sealed effectively with acrylic gesso.

New Decorative Materials

In traditional decoupage, it is important to imbed the decorative paper under many coats of varnish. Consequently, only thin papers are used, or heavier papers are thinned by peeling away their undersides. However, the constraints of this particular style need not impose themselves on other creative efforts so long as the finish is reasonably protective. Durability is relative, and may not always be a prime consideration.

The thickness and composition of decorative materials can be varied to include:

fabrics, ribbons and lace of all kinds, foils, wood and other plant fibers (e.g., veneer, bark, pulp, cornhusks, grasses, seed pods and spores), all sorts of papers (e.g., handmade, tissue, embossed, composite), natural materials (e.g., leaves, flowers, feathers, insect wings, eggshells, mother-of-pearl flakes, mica)

These materials can be cut and arranged in their natural shapes or styled as mosaics and inlay. Where there are delicate or unusual textures, take care in sealing and finishing the design.

Photographs, postcards, and all the images on heavy paper stock can be cut out and pasted *without* thinning, but be sure to paste and seal them thoroughly. Actually, these thicker materials are preferable for another offshoot of decoupage known as "elevated." Since the term decoupage refers primarily to cutting, these images are released from their backgrounds and mounted three-dimensionally, usually inside a shadow box frame with raised glass. Because of their stiffness, these cutouts can be creased and molded, adding even more dimension. Since thicker materials can be considered for decoupage, don't dismiss the possibility of embellishing with all sorts of three-dimensional objects, exploring the realm of "collage."

With the advent of photocopying—now black & white, color and to scale—decoupage enters a new age of accessibility and creativity. Almost any image can now be quickly and cheaply reproduced, altered, manipulated, cut out and used as decoupage. Wherever such boundaries fall, the artistry of decoupage is enhanced.

New Finishing Techniques

There are some interesting new finishes to add to the old list of varnish, shellac and lacquer. The most notable among these is water-base polyurethane. It dries in less than an hour, doesn't yellow, and is very durable. By using exclusively water-base paints, sealants and glues, the entire decoupage process is quickened considerably all the way through finishing. Oil-base polyurethane can also be used, and will yellow over time producing that antique glow that is sometimes desirable.

There are several epoxy varnishes, resins and coatings that are also quick and extremely durable. Read all the instructions on the product label before deciding to use any of these, and experiment on a sample first. For a light finish, several coats of acrylic spray can be quite effective and easy to use.

One of the more unusual techniques that can be used to finish decoupage on glass is called "moonstone." The design cutouts are pasted on a mirror, then brushed with several coats of unthinned white glue, which is allowed to dry between coats. The ripply surface is finished with three coats of gloss varnish, then steel wooled and waxed. The effect is lunar magic.

An iridescent finish can be achieved on glass by applying pearl paint or spray on top. Designs are pasted underneath to show through, then painted on the underside with white or metallic paint. Silver or gold foil can be used instead of paint underneath.

Glass can also be smoked. Spray clear acrylic on the underside, let dry, hold it over a candle until a smoky film accumulates to your liking, then seal it with another coat of spray. Cutouts are pasted on a mirror surface, dried, and the smoky pane is then placed, smoke down, over top.

You may want to add "fly specks" for an antique effect. These can be spattered on lightly using a brush with a soft drab color.

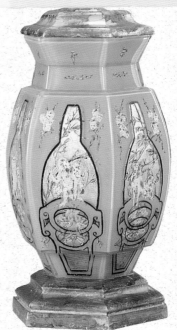

Potichomania lamp, by Cynthia Alderdice

Other sorts of texturing and faux finishes may occasionally be used to enhance a piece. Always experiment before attempting an unusual technique on a piece in which you've already invested much time.

Potichomania lamp, by Cynthia Alderdice

33

P r o j e c t s

Elementary Decoupage

DECORATOR TILE

A large terra-cotta tile makes a natural hot pad while complementing the hues of this peach cutout. Simply glue it in place and coat it with polyurethane.

OP ART BOX

Here's an ingenious way to adorn most any surface. This box is covered entirely with a large photocopy of folded fabric. Simple, yet effective.

WRAPPED FRAME

The frame of this lovely mirror piece is wrapped in overlapping strips of rice paper. A diluted wash of blue acrylic is sponged on and dried before gluing the strips with diluted white glue. A clear acrylic mat spray is used over top.

35

ALPHABET BLOCKS

These simple wooden blocks are transformed into ornamental playthings with hand-colored alphabets. The letters are photocopied to scale from art books. A tough finish ensures their longevity as childhood mementos.

36

BUILDING BLOCKS

Architectural shapes cut from wood form this classic set of building blocks. Scaled photocopies of old temples are applied to this set, but you may prefer to create different effects with other styles. This simple process can produce many fascinating results.

FLORAL BOXES

Bold floral cutouts grace the large, painted metal box, while nasturtium and morning glory patterns cover the upper and lower sections of the small filing box entirely. Any motif you use can evoke a specific use.

PLANTER AND SEED BOX

The colorful blossoms that festoon this planter eliminate the need to grow anything other than greenery, imparting their own everlasting cheer. The application of a seed packet to the little box is both functional and attractive.

GARDENING TOOL BOX

This old shoe shine box is converted to a gardening carry-all with the application of vintage seed packets. A polyurethane finish is prudent for outdoor use.

HOLIDAY ORNAMENTS

Byzantine images applied to wooden cutouts make colorful holiday ornaments for tree-trimming or hung on doors, walls or windows. They also make special gifts, and can be varied to suit any occasion.

HOLIDAY BASKET

Spray paint a simple mushroom basket, cut strips of wrapping paper or fabric with pinking shears and *voila*, you have a container for Christmas cards, or greens with cones and balls, or a wine and cheese basket. Alter the motif, and the possibilities increase.

40

ANTIQUE ROUND AND MUSIC BOXES

The round box acquires an antique character with the simple application of this medieval rondelle and faux bronze finish. The little music box is appropriately adorned with a cherub, gold braid and a strip of sheet music.

41

OFFICE TRAY

Tired of tasteful mahogany,
or worse, battleship gray in-out
trays in your office? You can liven
things up with cutouts from wrapping
paper, stickers, or any images that strike
your fancy.

42

CANDLE COLUMN

This over-size candlestick becomes a decorator's accent piece with its marbleized paper-covered column. The foundation block has a color-complementary antique print trimmed with gold ribbon.

Collage Decoupage

WOODLAND BOX

A child might enjoy creating this wood-land box to store the treasures they collect on hikes. Cardboard foundations can be reinforced with a coat of gesso. Plant material such as leaves, wild grass or husks are pressed and dried before gluing them down flat. The fabric and plastic imitations shown here are easier to use and will last indefinitely. Acrylic paint can be sponged on to unify the texture of the design. Use ample coats of finish when incorporating natural materials.

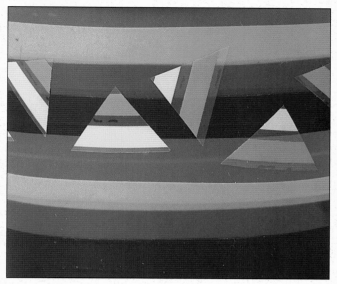

FLOWER POTS

Colored plastic tape and scissors are all you need to jazz up plastic flower pots. The color schemes and patterns of shapes you cut can be varied to suit almost any decor.

PEDESTAL PLANTER

The fabric leaves used to sheathe this dramatic pedestal planter are pre-coated with a protective finish. The edges won't unravel, they are easy to cut and paste, and they take a finish well. The pot is covered separately and left unattached.

SPOON RACK

Want to add a little color to something drab? A whole rainbow of possibilities are waiting for you at any paint store. Collect whatever color samples you like, cut and arrange them into an attractive pattern. Pinking shears made this project quick and easy to do.

CUTTING BOARD

A candy apple cutting board with its knife handle stem is even more fanciful covered in cutout fruits. These must be glued down securely and covered with several coats of tough polyurethane to withstand the blade, or the piece could be wall-mounted as a knife holder.

46

SERVING TRAYS

Ordinary plastic serving trays come alive with colorful images cut out of printed fabric (shown here), wall paper, or most anywhere else you find them. The trick is to apply a finish that will be waterproof and durable, in this case polyurethane.

47

CACHE BOX

Collect the holes punched out of colored foil papers for this glitzy cache box. Brush glue all over the box, dip it into the punched holes and let dry. Fill any spaces with stick-on stars, adding glue where necessary. Squirt glitter-filled glue around the shapes. Finish the edge of the lid with a strip of foil cut with pinking shears.

Certain stamps may have little philatelic value, but you save them because they're beautiful, interesting, or from faraway places. The collage on this box resulted from rummaging through old letters in an attic.

STAMP BOX

COLOR-WEAVE BOX

To achieve this effect, scribble all sorts of patterns on paper with felt tip marking pencils. Cut one sheet into narrow strips using a paper cutter, weave and glue them to the top of the box, then cut and paste different shaped sections to the sides.

CONFETTI BOX

This box is brushed with glue and dipped into shredded paper confetti. The striped motif is photocopied, punched with a hole puncher and cut with pinking shears. Dots of glitter-filled glue form the studs on top.

CARD BOX

If you're not playing with a full deck, rather than discard the remainder why not save face by giving a new box the royal treatment? The card stock can be thinned to wrap around edges, and image size can be altered with a color photocopier.

CASSETTE CASE & COVERS

Large, colored music notes are inked over scraps of sheet music to paper over this polka-dotted cassette case. The cassette cover inserts are redecorated with decoupage of magazine scraps, creating customized labels for specially dubbed recordings.

50

COLLAGE PINS

Fabulous collage pins like these are easy enough for a child to make. The foundations are cut from mat board and have clasp pins glued to their backs. The cutouts can be assembled in miniature (like these shown actual size) or at a larger scale and reduced on a color photocopier before gluing to the foundation. Finish the pin completely on all surfaces with several coats of clear acrylic. Consider incorporating a photo silhouette of a loved one for a personalized gift.

51

PHOTO ALBUMS

Unique design motifs can be added inside and out to notebooks or, as shown here, photo albums. The larger album incorporates wallpaper cutouts trimmed with ribbon, while the smaller one is composed of old photos and geometric shapes of tinted acetate. Notice how design elements can be carried throughout each page, creating continuity for a unified collage.

52

JOURNAL COVER

This unusual, open-spine journal features cutouts of significance to its owner. It is tied together visually under a veil of rice paper. The solid gold and zigzag borders accentuate the ethereal haze of the collage texture.

DESIGNER BOOKENDS

Strips of printed wrapping paper cut with pinking shears form the background of these bookends. Paisley and chevrons of silver, gold and black are cut and pasted over top, then trimmed with a bead of glitter-filled glue. Silver and gold braided tape is glued around the edge, which is painted with black dots to complete the ornamentation.

53

COLLAGE STOOL

With the exacting patience of masterful decoupage, this stool proves how a common object can be transformed into a work of art. Photocopies of interesting images (in this case, fabrics, natural textures, technical diagrams, cartoons, even kitchen utensils) are cut out and arranged in collage over the entire surface area. A methylan cellulose wallpaper glue can be used, along with polyurethane for finishing.

CHINA BOX

For an interesting variation of the photocopy method, these images of travel memorabilia are printed directly onto rice paper. (Use a sufficient weight of paper that won't get mangled in the machine.) The coin images are pasted onto cardboard cutouts for relief. The piece can be finished with several coats of varnish, before and after gluing on the cardboard coins.

STAR CLOCK

Stick-on vinyl letters and numbers decorate this clock in an abstract fashion. The stars are hand cut from vinyl. The stars that mark the dial are phosphorescent. Of course, your clock might want to put on a different face.

CITY LIGHTS

After a base coat of midnight blue, this lamp is prepared for "putting on the Ritz." Switch on the street lamp over a starry night in Manhattan, or any other scene you'd like to depict. Decoupage shapes are cut from adhesive-backed paper and stuck on the shade, spray painted, then removed.

55

WORLDS OF ART

Plastic or wooden croquet balls serve as fascinating foundations, much the way eggs have been artfully decorated down through the ages. Start with a base coat of gesso and sand smooth. These images are cut from the pages of tool catalogs, then dipped in pigmented watercolors. The cutouts are applied over a wet coat of clear acrylic gloss medium which has been brushed onto the ball. After drying, two or three coats of a clear acrylic mat finish go over top and can be blotted as necessary with a cotton ball.

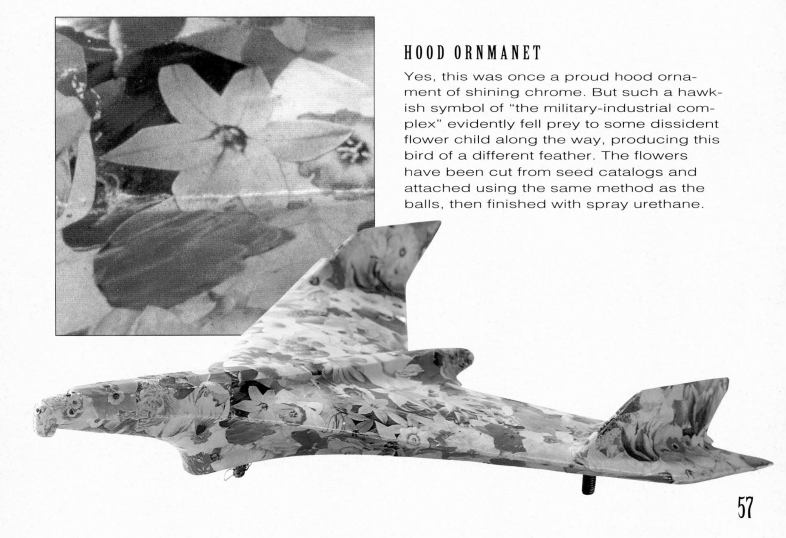

HOOD ORNMANET

Yes, this was once a proud hood ornament of shining chrome. But such a hawkish symbol of "the military-industrial complex" evidently fell prey to some dissident flower child along the way, producing this bird of a different feather. The flowers have been cut from seed catalogs and attached using the same method as the balls, then finished with spray urethane.

COLLECTOR PLATES

Simple plates become collector's items when decorated with decoupage and other assorted design elements. Shapes cut from mat board, along with various trinkets, elevate these collages into the third dimension. The design elements used here include computer laser images, color photocopies, leaves, shredded paper, oriental handmade papers, comic strips, newspaper advertisements and toy animals.

59

COLLAGE FEMME

Decoupage techniques are utilized in both the collages shown here. Paper images cut from greeting cards, wrapping paper, seed packets, and magazines are pasted on a board, along with doilies, lace and silk flowers. Three dimensional objects like the fan and string of pearls can be attached with a glue gun.

60

COLLAGE ATHLETIQUE

Not that we're promoting stereotypes, but this collage might be more welcome in a boy's room. It's a great way to encourage tidiness the next time he needs to pick up all those stray magazines, trading cards and ballpark souvenirs. He might even enjoy making this himself.

Traditional Decoupage

Jewelry Box

■ The base coat for this little jewelry box is a faux finish of flame tortoise. A matching pigskin is used for the lining. If you are not familiar with gold leafing technique, you can substitute gold foil paper.

1. Sand and seal the box.

2. Lay aluminum leaf over the outside of the box and inside lip of top and bottom.

3. Seal the leaf with an equal mixture of denatured alcohol and shellac.

4. Prepare a mixture of one part asphaltum to two parts varnish.

5. Using a Number 6 or 8 round watercolor brush, lay radials in amorphous strokes on the box.

6. Immediately whisk away the ends of the radials lightly with a cotton ball that has been dipped in flatting oil, in order to vary the transparency. About 60 percent of the background is covered with these radials. Think of a tortoise shell, and you can visualize how the radials should look. Allow to dry and seal with diluted shellac.

7. Mix a glaze of alizarin crimson: one part alizarin crimson tube oil paint to two parts quick drying varnish to one part turpentine. Layer with several coats of this glaze until you have the desired transparency and depth of color. Allow the piece to dry thoroughly.

8. Varnish with enough coats to bury the radials of asphaltum.

9. To create prints, lay white gold leaf on tacky gold leaf quick size which has been applied to translucent drafting paper. Seal with an equal mixture of denatured alcohol and shellac.

10. Cut prints out creatively without drawing the design on the paper or using patterns. Just cut!

11. Arrange and glue the prints down on the box.

12. Varnish 20 coats or more. Wet sand with #220, then #400 and #600 sandpapers after every 10 coats.

13. Rub by hand or with #0000 steel wool, then wax.

Pillement Box

■ This charming round box is decorated with gold leaf silhouettes from prints by Jean Pillement. Again, gold foil paper may be substituted for the gold leaf.

1. Sand, seal and paint the exterior with red oil paint.

2. Lay gold leaf size and leaf on the interior of the box and lid. Varnish and sand until smooth.

3. Seal the back side of the uncut print with acrylic spray or a lightly brushed-on equal mixture of denatured alcohol and shellac.

4. The gold leaf will be applied to the wrong side of the uncut black and white print.

5. Brush gold leaf size on the paper. At the proper tack, lay on the gold leaf. Use your knuckle to test the degree of tack of the size. A dry tack is what you want in order to lay the leaf, not a real wet tack. Be sure that you overlap the pieces of leaf slightly. Smooth and push down the gold leaf into the size with a tamper brush or a very soft bristle brush. When dry, brush off your skewings and seal with an equal mixture of white shellac and denatured alcohol.

6. Cut out the prints on the right side following the black lines of the prints, then glue the right side down onto the box with the gold leaf facing up. Clean away excess glue.

7. Varnish until the prints are buried. Wet sand with #220, then #400 and #600 sand-papers.

8. Rub by hand or with #0000 steel wool, then wax.

64

Yatsuhashi Box

■ "Yatsuhashi" means zig-zag bridge, and is the name of a place in Aichi-Prefecture in Japan that has been famous since ancient times for its irises. The bridge and iris motif has inspired many artists in creating objets d'art. This inkstone gold lacquered box is a reproduction of such a piece.

Like many of the foundation objects used in projects throughout this book, this box is highly specialized. When recreating a unique project, you can either construct a matching foundation or look for one that is similar. The box and stand shown here are made from scratch out of walnut.

1. Prime and paint the box with up to a dozen coats of black acrylic.

2. Paint 3 coats of acrylic "red clay" bole (see instructions on page 102. on one side of some translucent architectural drafting paper.

3. Seal the paper with clear acrylic spray, and let dry thoroughly.

4. Apply gold leaf size to the bole, let dry to tack, then lay on gold leaf. Tamp it down with a soft brush and gently burnish.

5. All the iris leaves are creatively cut from this paper.

6. Paper for the bridge is prepared the same way, only brushed with acids or covered with silver leaf to vary the hue.

7. The iris flowers are cut from mother-of-pearl which is first softened by soaking in the hottest water from your tap.

8. When pasting down the mother-of-pearl, use white glue. Clean up excess glue with paper towels moistened with warm water.

9. Apply ten coats of varnish with a sponge brush before dry sanding with #400, then #600 sandpapers. Repeat this process three times.

10. After five more coats, wet sand with the same two grits. For a final sheen, rub on talcum powder with a cloth soaked in mineral oil, then with toothpaste, then wax.

11. The stand can be sanded, stained, then finished with varnish and wax.

Tea Chest Boxes

66

Umbrella Stand

67

Tea Chest Boxes

■ Both of the tea chest boxes (on page 66) are covered with silver tea chest paper. The decoupage that decorates each one, however, is quite different. The box with human figures is decorated with simulated Japanese wood-block prints, while the fans and bamboo on the other box are cut from specially prepared papers known as "carta metallica."

Either box begins the same way:

1. Sand and seal the box, then sand again lightly for a smooth surface.

2. Using a polymer medium or glue of your choice, cover the box with silver tea chest paper, burnish with a dry cloth and let dry.

To decorate with prints, continue:

3. Color the prints with oil pencils if they are black and white. A tortillon dipped in turpentine can be used to blend these colors to simulate a Japanese wood-block print.

4. Seal the prints and let dry.

5. Cut out the prints to suit your design.

6. Glue the prints in place, clean away any excess glue, and let dry.

To decorate with carta metallica, continue:

3. Brush gold leaf quick size onto translucent drafting paper. Let dry to a dry tack. Lay gold, silver, copper and composition leaf onto the size and burnish with a soft brush.

4. The effect of different metals with dimensional shading is created by applying various stains, tarnishing agents (such as cupric nitrate, barium sulfide, potassium sulfide, sodium sulfide), aniline dyes, paints and other miscellaneous solutions. Experiment to create your own effects.

5. Seal the paper with an equal mixture of denatured alcohol and white shellac.

6. Cut out your own shapes free form for your design. Glue them down, clean away any excess glue and let dry.

To finish either box:

7. Apply many more coats of water base varnish than it takes to bury the decoupage.

8. Wet sand with #220, then #400 and #600 sandpapers. Rub by hand or with #0000 steel wool, then wax. The fine patina will accentuate the metallic papers.

9. The base can be rubbed with teakwood stain, then waxed.

Umbrella Stand

■ The umbrella stand (on page 67) is decorated in the same manner as the tea chest box with simulated Japanese woodblock prints. The only difference is that these prints are not buried in varnish. Since the piece is much larger and more utilitarian, the main criteria for finishing is that it be adequately protected and durable rather than a labor intensive work of art.

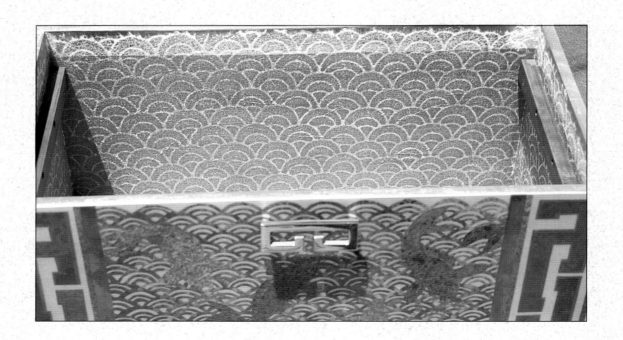

Voyager Chest

Voyager Chest

■ The voyager chest (on pages 70 and 71) is yet another example of the elegant oriental style that has captivated decoupeurs for centuries. Simply by shifting continents or periods of art history, many more wonderful designs can be executed.

1. This chest is custom made out of pine. The stand is made of walnut.

2. Sand and seal the chest inside and out. Lightly sand the exterior again for extra smoothness.

3. Using a water base varnish or glue of your choice, cover the box with silver tea chest paper, burnish and let dry.

4. Create a variety of carta metallica papers using the method described for the tea chest (on page 68). Sort out these papers for use as contrasting elements of the design you have planned, such as shades of water, fish and border motifs.

5. Three different shades of carta metallica are used for the water pattern on the lid of this chest. Parts of the pattern can be cut free form using scissors or an X-acto knife.

6. The fish are cut from reddish copper carta metallica to resemble carp. Mother-of-pearl is glued behind the fish, as well as the moon and highlights on the ocean waves.

7. Before gluing the pieces down, you can position them with sticky tack to ensure proper design placement. An equal mixture of white glue and harrower's glue works well. Let dry thoroughly.

8. Ten coats of a water base varnish can be applied before wet sanding with #400-600 papers. Apply five more coats, then sand again.

9. The interior of this chest is painted with a clay-colored acrylic, then sealed with water base varnish.

10. Rice paper with a water pattern is applied over a wet coat of water base varnish or diluted glue. After drying, it is sealed with two coats of water base varnish.

11. After several weeks of drying, buff the exterior with #0000 steel wool, then polish one or more times with wax.

12. The stand is rubbed with a teak wood stain, then waxed.

Oriental Scroll

■ The oriental scroll (on page 74) features an original design using carta metallica papers. Fabric is seldom used as a foundation because of its flexibility, but does not pose a problem here since the scroll remains static when hung on a wall.

If you do not find a blank scroll to use as your foundation, one can be made quite simply using wooden dowels and two or three contrasting shades of silk fabric. The two border shades of silk used here are woven with a pattern of gold, while the background is plain.

1. Cut a panel of heavy paper or stiffened canvas to use as the backing. Cut and paste each section of fabric in place, folding the margins either around the backing or under themselves for finished edges. You may want to stain the fabric with tea before assembling, to achieve an antique effect. Lightly iron the piece at various stages of assembly. Cut and paint the dowels, then glue the fabric around them at the top and bottom.

2. Create a variety of carta metallica papers using the method described for the tea chest (on page 68).

3. After sealing the papers, cut whatever shapes you desire for your design. These can be cut free form in a creative manner.

4. Glue the shapes onto the fabric, being careful not to use excessive glue which could make messy edges. After drying, seal with clear acrylic spray.

Bristol Egg

■ Hand colored prints of cherubs and meandering scrolls embellish the glass Bristol egg (on page 75). Tinted foils illuminate sections of mother-of-pearl for further enhancement. The stand was inspired by an antique, reproduced here as a hybrid of various found objects.

1. If a glass egg is not easily obtainable, look for a plastic one which can be painted if necessary. Prepare the surface.

2. Color, seal and cut out the prints. These can be temporarily held in place with sticky tack during the gluing process for proper positioning.

3. Cut mother-of-pearl into desired shapes to fit over and under the print or alone. Mother-of-pearl will soften in hot water and then may be cut with scissors.

Tinted foils for illumination may be glued to the back of the pearl and then cut out with scissors.

4. Glue all pieces on the egg. Be extremely careful that all excess glue is cleaned from the print and the egg before varnishing.

5. Varnish the egg. You will need many more coats of varnish for covering the mother-of-pearl than you need for plain prints.

6. Wet sand with #400-#600 papers. Rub with #0000 steel wool, then wax.

7. The stand can be glued together using epoxy. Look for old lamp fixtures, a plant hanger hook, lathe turned dowels and large wooden beads with pre-drilled holes. Finish with metallic paint and faux antiquing. A clear gloss finish adds sheen.

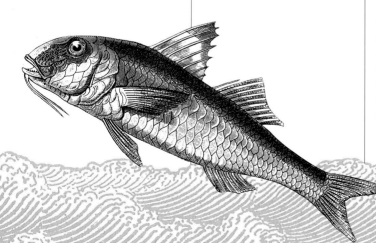

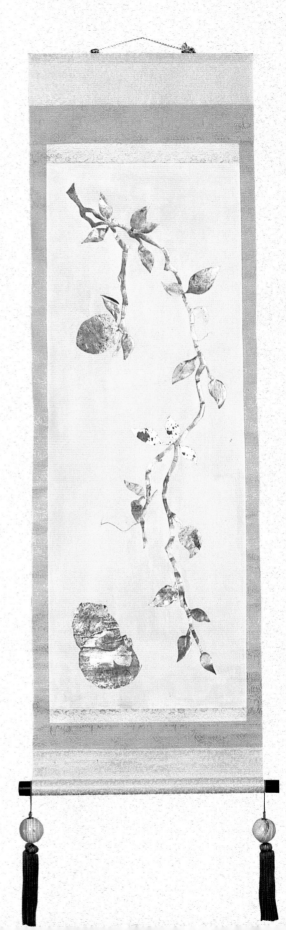

Oriental Scroll

Bristol Egg

Game Table

■ The spectacular game table (on page 78) is custom made from solid walnut. You could achieve a similar effect by decorating a pre-existing table top instead. By varying the design pattern, you can create almost any kind of game table you like.

1. Most sections of this table receive two base coats of black oil paint. The entire surface is sealed with clear varnish.

2. The border of gold can be cut from gold teapaper with an X-acto knife and a straight edge, then glued in place.

3. Gold braid is glued around the edges of the cups and along the outlines of the concentric squares.

4. The prints are all colored with oil pencils and sealed before cutting.

5. Mother-of-pearl is integrated with the prints when they are glued down, sometimes over and sometimes under portions of the print. Soak the mother-of-pearl in hot water before cutting out its shapes.

6. Squares of tea-paper are used to checker the center, along with mother-of-pearl cut to match the border pattern. Glue them securely, then wipe away any excess glue.

7. At least 20 coats of varnish should be applied. Depending on its intended use, a table could be given added protection by substituting polyurethane or epoxy resin.

8. When varnishing, wet sand after every ten coats with #400-600 papers. Buff and wax.

Yatsuhashi Screen

■ Screen panels have long been a favorite project of decoupeurs. The Japanese iris screen (on page 79) celebrates the traditional Yatsuhashi bridge and iris motif.

1. The screen is constructed with four panels of 12" x 36" tempered masonite. They are sealed with orange shellac on both sides and hinged on the back side with fabric cut on the bias. Two layers of fabric are glued down with white glue.

2. The panels are then covered with gold chinese tea-paper treated with aniline and cut 3" smaller than the panels. They are glued down with water base varnish.

3. The borders are made from crino-line. Gold leaf size is applied on the crinoline, and variegated leaf is applied to give a fabric effect. The crinoline is glued down on the outer edge of the screen with white glue.

4. Japanese wood-block prints of irises and butterflies are used, and can be supplemented with blank pieces of paper which are colored and creatively cut for extra leaves and buds. Seal the prints before cutting.

5. The bridge across the screen is made from carta metallica paper (see instructions for tea chest on page 68). In this case, sodium sulfide is applied to the dutch metal with cotton batting, then black aniline dye.

6. The beams supporting the bridge are made from a differently pre-pared carta metallica. Using a toothbrush, spatter black aniline dye and orange glass stain over the dutch metal leaf. Seal all the carta metallica papers with two coats of water base varnish.

7. Sticky tack can be used to hold all the cutouts in place while arranging the design. After they are all glued down, use a damp cloth to wipe away any excess glue.

8. Seven coats of water base varnish are then applied to the screen area, but not to the variegated crinoline.

9. The biggest problem is keeping the paper in the folds of the screen from cracking and splitting, since the screen must be folded and unfolded so many times. This can be remedied by adding an extra layer of teapaper down the folds.

10. The back of the four panel screen is covered with silk on rice paper and quickly glued down with white glue. (If you work with it too long, the rice paper and silk have a tendency to stretch.)

11. Brasses can be added to the corners, edges and top of the screen to complete the oriental appearance.

Screen of Fans

■ The screen of fans (on page 79) is yet another variation on an oriental design.

1. The frame for this screen is made of solid walnut. It is a three panel screen of masonite boards sealed with one coat of varnish front and back.

2. The panels are covered with gold leafed silk paper, then glued with white glue on the front side of the masonite.

3. Each fan is individually designed using handcolored prints, mother-of-pearl, construction paper, chinese teapaper, rice paper, silver and gold leaf.

4. After designing each fan separately, they are placed on the screen and glued down. The prints will resist the silk gold leaf paper, but with persistence and heavy books as weights, they will adhere.

5. A clear gloss varnish is applied to the panels. They are sanded with #400-600 wet sandpaper between each ten coats of varnish. When about 35 coats of varnish have been applied, a final sanding is done and then the piece is waxed for a final polishing.

6. The back of the screen can be covered with silk rice paper. The screen is then hinged.

Yatsuhashi Screen

Elevated Decoupage

This style of decoupage emphasizes the aspect of cutting. One or more layers of stiffened paper are raised and mounted above a background. If a print is on paper that is too thin, it can be pasted to a stiffer sheet before it is sealed and cut.

Decoupage Mat

■ The little mirror (opposite) gets a grand treatment with delicate cuttings that seem to hover over the extra wide mat.

1. The frame, mirror, glass, mat and beveled gold strip are all standard items available at most any picture framing shop.

2. Color, seal and cut the print.

3. Place the cutouts over the mat and mirror. Any portion of the design that is over the mirror will have to be blacked out so as not to reflect in the mirror. Do this by using a black felt tip marker with the print face down on a piece of wax paper.

4. Place the design carefully over the mat and mirror, deciding exactly where it will be placed. Carefully, using a toothpick, dab a heavy glue on the underside of the print and place it back into position on the mat, making sure that it is well connected at various points.

5. Carefully clean up any glue spots with a damp paper towel. Extra prints can be added if messy spots need to be covered.

6. Place the glass over top and install the piece into its frame.

Decoupage Fan

■ The Brussels lace of the wedding fan (opposite) serves as an elegant way to lift these oriental Pillement designs above their background. The shadow box frame is a standard item that can be ordered through custom picture framing shops.

1. Fasten the fan to its background.

2. These prints are hand colored with oil pencils using shades within the chinoiserie palette.

3. Seal the prints thoroughly before cutting them out, then arrange them until the design is most pleasing.

4. Apply a good fabric glue to the entire surface of the back side of each cutout, and glue them into place. Be careful not to allow any excess glue to seep beyond the edges of the cutout onto the fabric of the fan, but make sure all the edges are glued down.

5. Install the piece under glass in its frame.

High Fashion

■ These ladies assume an elevated status through raised decoupage integrated with fabric, ribbon and beads. Their finery remains protected under the glass of a shallow shadow box frame.

1. You will need two of any print you decide to fashion. One is selectively cut for the raised elements, while the other serves as the background. If the paper isn't already rather stiff, paste both prints onto backing sheets. Seal both prints.

2. Decide which areas of the figure you want to decorate with fabric before deciding which will be cut out and raised. Cut out the raised elements and reposition them over the background as you gradually integrate the fabric and other materials.

3. Sheer fabric can be gathered and pulled through holes or slits in the background. A needle and thread will secure the gathers where necessary. Excess fabric is secured

with tape wherever it is pulled through the background (as shown in the photo). The fabric should be "poofed" out and arranged before taping. Try to pull the fabric through holes in areas where the raised decoupage cutouts or other decorative elements will cover them.

4. Continue redressing the figure with all sorts of fabrics, lace, ribbons, beads or other materials. A fabric glue will aid in this process, but should never be visible.

5. The decoupage cutouts are sometimes glued into place as you attach the fabric, but generally are glued on last. Use a good fabric glue.

Pansies & Ladies of the Court

■ Both of these pieces are brought to life with multiple layers of prints, each cut with a creative sense of which features will appear in the back, middle and foreground. Each layer is attached over the preceding layer, either with glued stacks of cardboard "feet," or with generous globs of silicone sealant. These must always be placed behind the largest areas of a cutout where they will not be seen.

Many of the cutouts are often contoured as well, and can be molded into realistic shapes in the moist, warm hollows of your hand. This is one way decoupage reaches creatively into the next dimension.

The picture of pansies is constructed out of five layers. The ladies of the court (opposite) use eight. In either case, you should:

1. Paste the bottom print to a cardboard backing.

2. Seal all the prints for stiffness. You may even reseal lightly after contouring in order to help hold the shape.

3. Generally, each new layer is cut from less of the print to reveal parts of the layer below.

4. Certain layers may be anchored at the side and extend in toward the center of the piece.

85

Cherubs & The Garden

■ Both the cherubs and garden are elevated treatments the French called "vue d'optique." The cherubs are highlighted with gold foil illumination added to the colored prints. The garden utilizes a full palette of 18th century colors. Both pieces are lined with moire silk, which is wrapped around panels of mat board and installed, side panels first, then the bottom.

Each layer of decoupage is glued onto supportive members: either stacks of cardboard, toothpicks or wires. These must never be visible, yet they must be fastened quite securely.

Neither of these pieces uses double images like those in the last two projects. Each of these images is cut once only and remains distinct, delicate and airy.

Repoussé

The distinctive feature of repoussé, which simply means "to raise up," is the filling of an embossed image on heavy paper to achieve solid relief. This has also been called "moulage" and "paper tole." If a print is too thin, it can be pasted to a backing sheet before embossing. Fabric can also be used.

The embossed cavities can be filled with various supportive materials: paper-mâché, salt dough, tissues mixed with mucilage, French clay, cornstarch clay, styrofoam, silicone or whatever other stable material you may find. If the embossed attachments are too delicate, they can always be protected under raised glass.

Table Screen

■ The oriental table screen (opposite) features a shallow relief image on both sides. The background and frame are covered with silver and composition leaf. The foundation is best custom cut and built in a wood shop.

1. Sand well and seal, then size and lay leaf on the screen. Composition leaf has been laid on the frame and silver leaf on the background. (This leaf has been tarnished using the methods of gilding found in *The Art of Painted Finish* by Isabel O'Neil.)

2. Cut out the print and seal. For repoussé, you will need more than one print in order to achieve realistic dimensions and levels.

3. Coat the underside of each print that has been separately cut out with glue. Smooth a thin layer of stuffing material to the back side of the print.

4. Lay the concave side of each piece on wax paper to shape and mold the outside of the print in a realistic manner. Be careful not to damage the print. When the print is dry, glue it to the screen.

5. In the same way, add other pieces of prints: a fold of skirt, an arm, leg, hair, scarf, etc. You can achieve a very realistic look by using many pieces, but carefully study your print to know what pieces to use below and on top of each other before cutting them out and gluing them down. If you have a figure in the background, glue it down first.

6. Varnish and finish the piece (without waxing) before applying subsequent pieces for repoussé. Always bury the prints and finish the background before beginning to repoussé.

7. Finish the repoussé with a rub of #0000 steel wool. Then the whole piece is buffed and waxed.

89

Pieck Purse

■ This purse is a classic example of high relief repoussé. It showcases a panoramic treatment of prints by Anton Pieck. Of course, designs and foundations can be varied extensively with this basic technique.

1. Sand the raw wood foundation, then you can either seal, stain and seal, or seal and paint.

2. You will need two of any print you use. Seal them. Cover the box with one set of prints by cutting them to fit and gluing them into place.

3. The relief portions of the second set of prints are cut out, molded and filled the same as the preceding project. Allow ample drying time for the filled shape to stabilize, and refill if there is significant shrinkage.

4. Glue each piece of relief into place with a glue that is appropriate to your filler as well as the paper, and let dry thoroughly. Trim various edges with gold braid, ribbon or decorative fabric tape.

5. Varnish 10-20 coats. Always use steel wool over any contoured areas after every five coats. Flat areas can be sanded in the usual manner. Finish with wax over the entire exterior. Polyurethane can be substituted for extra durability, but will not produce the same finesse.

6. Cut and glue a lining of your choice to the interior. Trim any unfinished edges with ribbon or tape.

7. Install hardware such as hinges, clasps and handles.

91

Two repoussé boxes, by Helen La Rose

Potichomania

Potichomania is derived from the French word *Potichimanie* (*potiche* meaning oriental vase and *manie* referring to mania). This art form was practiced in mid-19th century England where it became known as Potichomania, referring to the craze of decorating clear glass vases with cutout prints.

The favorite type of urn used was the clear glass shape with at least one opening allowing the artist to position and glue colorful cut prints to the inside of the piece. The inside of the vase was then painted, which gave the illusion of fine porcelain. Since the shapes resembled actual vases, flowers were arranged in them and, of course, water was needed. The destructive effect of the water on the prints may be one reason why there are so few samples of these old Potichomania vases in existence.

Potichomania plate, by Patricia Nimocks

Another reason is the fragile nature of the hand blown glass that was used. Because of the water problem, artists began working on the outside of the vases which resulted in a raised surface. Unfortunately, while this solved one problem, the finished product lost the elegant look of fine porcelain.

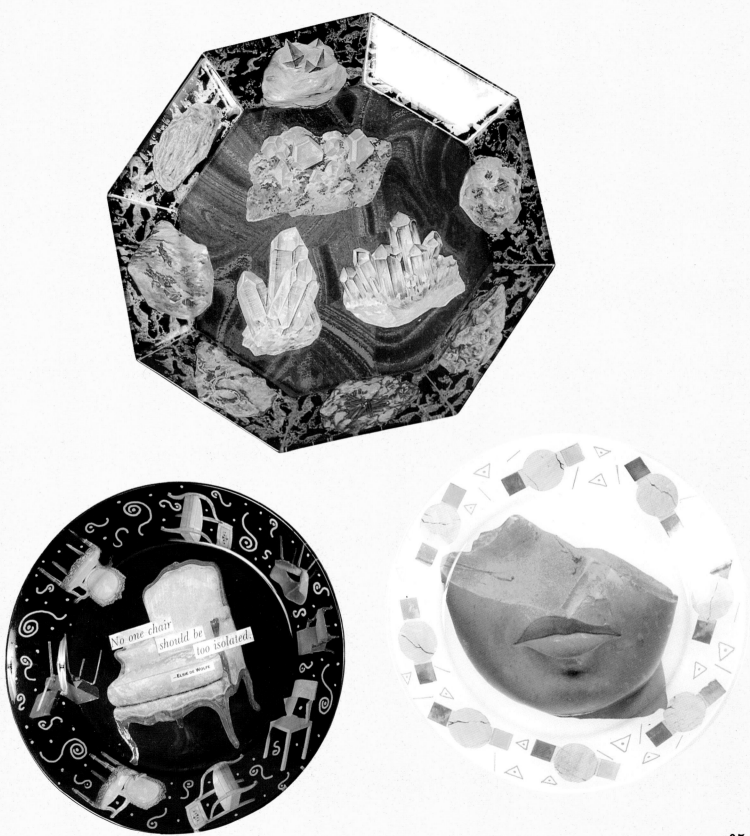

Potichomania plates, by Terry Taylor

Potichomania Plate

Materials Needed:

Clear Glass Plate or Cylinder

Prints

Slow-drying glue

Manicure scissors

X-acto knife

Sticky tack

Acrylic spray fixative

Sponge brush

Background paint, gold leaf or paper

Felt tip pen that writes on glass

1

2

3

4

96

Potichomania Plate

Potichomania has since experienced a revival. The following instructions for working on a flat clear glass plate incorporate the same techniques required to work inside a vase or lamp base. Once the gluing and background methods have been learned, it will be time to experience the thrill of creating a lasting piece of Potichomania.

1. Select suitable prints for the project (shown on pages 96-97).

2. Spray front and back of prints with acrylic spray fixative, preferably mat.

3. Cut intricate interior portions of the print with an X-acto knife, then cut the remainder with curved manicure scissors (see photo 1).

4. When all the prints are cut, place them on the top surface of the glass to determine the proper design (see photo 2). If it is a very detailed design, take a felt tip marker and trace around your design.

5. If there are several elements to the design, place small pieces of sticky tack to the back of the prints and press down on the top of the glass plate to hold the design in place.

6. Spread the slow-drying glue on the back of the plate, as if greasing a pan. A little glycerin added to the glue will slow the drying time. Always test on another piece of glass to make sure your mixture is right.

7. Transfer the print from the front of the glass plate to the back of the plate. Be sure to look at the front of the print while gluing. Work out the glue using a press and roll movement with your fingers. This holds the print in place while removing the glue from between the plate and the face of the print. *Always work so the face of the print is visible.*

8. Clean the plate using a dampened paper towel and cotton swabs. Be sure to thoroughly clean the glue from the entire glass surface.

9. When the print is dry, different backgrounds such as paint, gold leaf, and rice paper may be applied. If the background is to be painted behind the print, a second gluing will be necessary. Place undiluted glue on the tip of your finger and force glue under the edges of the print. If a gap is there, the glue will be seen going under the print. At that time press the print down until the glue dries completely. (If this step has not been done the paint will seep under the face of the print.)

10. When painting the background, alkyd flat oil base paint is recommended. Use a sponge brush in a patting motion. Let dry overnight. Apply a second coat of paint. Dry again overnight and then apply three or four coats of varnish (solvent turpentine). This step waterproofs the plates so they can be *hand washed.*

11. If using a rice paper backing, the second gluing (step 9) may be eliminated. Rice papers are available in many colors and types from art supply stores. White rice papers may also be colored using strong tea or coffee. Tear the rice paper in small pieces making sure there are no straight or cut edges. Spread glue on the back of the plate in small areas. Place the torn rice paper on the back of the plate and back of the print. Be sure to overlap the paper so no glass or back of print shows. Press out the glue from under the rice paper, then glue remaining areas of the plate. Let this first layer of rice paper dry (see photo 3). Apply a second layer, as before. A third layer of paper, such as gold tea chest paper (see photo 4) or paint may be applied to give the piece a more finished look. When thoroughly dry, apply three or four coats of varnish.

12. After each coat of varnish has dried overnight, the finish may be sanded gently using #400 wet/dry sandpaper which has been dampened with water.

13. The plates are now ready to use. However, they should be treated as any fine crystal or china. *Always wash by hand.*

Oriental Bowl

■ The gold bowl with oriental designs (on page 100) utilizes very much the same process as the plates. Since the surface of the bowl is more curved, choose designs without much surface area that will conform more readily without creasing.

1. Color, seal and cut out the designs.

2. Clean the glass thoroughly with vinegar and water to remove any dirt or oils.

3. Using a fingertip or a stiff brush, coat the entire image side of the cutouts with diluted white glue.

4. Press the cutouts gently into place on the outside of the bowl. Press out excess glue with a rolling motion of your fingers, then carefully wipe away excess with a damp towel. Let dry thoroughly.

5. Apply one coat of water base varnish over the outside of the bowl.

6. The outside of the bowl can be covered with any number of finishes: metallic paint, opaque colored paint, foil, rice paper, carta metallica paper, composition metallic leaf…whatever suits your design.

7. Apply several coats of varnish, then sand and wax to finish.

Oriental Bowl

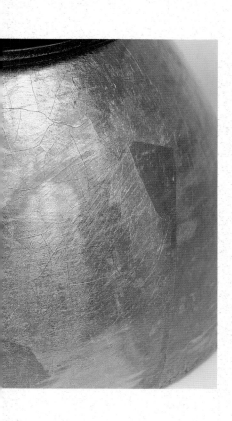

Pillement Lamp

101

Pillement Lamp

■ The gold silhouette lamp (on page 101) makes use of a unique process developed by the same artist who introduced carta metallica. In making this lamp, she applied gold leafed prints by Pillement over tarnished Dutch metal on the exterior of the glass cylinder.

1. Paint the outside of the glass cylinder with red bole:

> **2 volumes of red red orange Japan paint**
>
> **1 volume of burnt sienna Japan paint**
>
> **2 volumes of flat white oil paint**
>
> **1/2 volume of turpentine**
>
> **1/4 volume of flatting oil**

Seal with an equal mixture of shellac and denatured alcohol.

2. Lay size, then Dutch metal over the painted surface. Do not be concerned if the red shows through.

3. Tarnish the cylinder with a mixture of sodium sulfide (pea-sized piece to 1/2 cup of warm water). With a cottonball, dab this mixture on the Dutch metal. (Wear rubber gloves.) The Dutch metal will begin to change colors, moving from blue to purples. Do not leave this wet solution on the Dutch metal for too long or it will burn through the leaf. To stop this procedure, pat dry (do not rub) the wet solution on the cylinder. Dab with cold water and dry again.

4. Let dry overnight and seal the leafed area the next day with the shellac and denatured alcohol solution. (Note: a variation of this process would be to gesso the exterior of the glass, then paint it with metallic or other paint.)

5. Seal the back side of the uncut print with acrylic spray or a lightly brushed-on equal mixture of denatured alcohol and shellac.

6. The gold leaf will be applied to the wrong side of the uncut black and white print.

7. Brush gold leaf size on the paper. At the proper tack, lay on the gold leaf. Use your knuckle to test the degree of tack of the size. A dry tack is what you want in order to lay the leaf, rather than a wet tack. Be sure that you overlap the pieces of leaf slightly. Smooth and push down the gold leaf into the size with a tamper brush or a very soft bristle brush. When dry, brush off your skewings and seal with an equal mixture of white shellac and denatured alcohol.

8. Cut out the prints on the right side following the black lines of the prints, then glue the right side down onto the box.

9. Varnish with resin varnish to bury. Wet sand with #220, #400 and #600 sandpapers. The amount of varnish coats depends on the thickness of your print. Be sure you always use many more coats of varnish than to just bury the prints. The varnish will shrink in time, and it must be buried well if you desire a smooth finish. (Note: a variation of finishing would be to use epoxy, which is quick and very durable, and can also be used as adhesive to attach the cutouts.)

10. Rub well with your hand or #0000 steel wool, then wax.

Poppy Lamp

■ The black lamp with red poppies (on page 104) is decorated from the inside of the glass cylinder.

1. Color the poppy prints. If using watercolor, as shown here, they can be sealed with water base varnish.

2. Plan your design, then cut out all the shapes.

3. Using your finger or a stiff brush, apply diluted white glue to the entire image side of the cutouts. Glue them to the inside of the glass. Gently press out any excess glue and wipe it away carefully. Make sure all the edges are glued down securely so that the paint won't seep under them. Let dry thoroughly.

4. Paint the inside of the cylinder with black oil base paint. Do not brush the paint, as you may disturb the glued print and have black paint seeping under the prints. The best way to apply this paint is to use a sponge applicator and dab it onto the inside of the cylinder over the prints.

5. Allow the cylinder to dry on its side so that air may flow through both ends of the cylinder. Periodically rotate the cylinder on its side so that paint will not collect in one place while drying and cause cracking of the paint. Applying a touch up coat is preferable to one excessive coat that may pool up and crack.

Partridge Lamp

■ The partridge lamp (on page 104) is decorated using virtually the same process as was used for the black lamp with poppies.

Keep in mind these basic tips for successful poti-chomania:

1. Clean the glass with vinegar and water.

2. Seal the prints before cutting.

3. Apply glue over the entire image side of each cutout, and make sure all the edges are glued down. A barely damp sponge can be used to press them down flat.

4. Allow the cutouts to dry thoroughly.

5. A coat of water base varnish can be applied at this stage to further seal the edges of the prints with the glass.

6. Use a sponge applicator to paint the interior so as not to disturb the prints. Certain paints, such as metallic or translucent colors, will probably require more than one coat.

104

Eggshell Decoupage

This intriguing process is executed much the same as any mosaic. Once the shells are cleaned, they are crushed into relatively flat sections, colored or left natural, and glued to a background which is usually of contrasting color to enhance the effect. They can be used to fill outlined areas as a mosaic, or to fill an entire background as a unique texture, as shown here. Decoupage cutouts can be pasted over top of an eggshell background, or placed adjacent to sections of eggshell. Aside from cutting, eggshell requires essentially the same techniques and materials as any other decoupage.

Butterfly Lamp

■ The two projects which follow involve a process in which the shells are glued in a continuous mosaic onto paper. Shapes are then cut out and glued to a foundation in true decoupage fashion. The lamp (on page 108) features eggshell decoupage affixed to mirrors, with protective glass panels mounted over top.

1. The custom walnut lamp has pairs of parallel grooves cut into the corner members. The mirror and glass panels slide into these, forming the body of the lamp base.

2. When you have several dozen pre-washed eggshells saved up, soak them in an equal mixture of water and liquid bleach to remove all the membranes. Soak and rinse thoroughly with water, then let them dry.

3. Use oil paints to color about half the shells orange, a quarter black and a quarter creamy white. The color scheme can, of course, be varied.

4. Find four 12" x 12" sheets of mulberry rice paper, or the equivalent. Two sheets will be used for the orange shells, and one each for the black and cream. Paint these sheets with watered-down black acrylic paint.

5. Crush and glue eggshell fragments to the paper using tweezers to position them evenly in a tightly fitted pattern. A slightly diluted white glue or cricket cage glue is suitable. Wipe up excess glue with a damp cloth as you go. This is the most time-consuming phase of the project.

6. When each sheet is done, clean once more overall, gently wiping with a cloth dampened in warm water. Let dry.

7. Seal each sheet with a coat of water base varnish.

8. Find or draw the art deco patterns to aid in cutting the eggshell paper. The black-ened mulberry paper backing of these pieces will be glued directly to the mirror, reflecting black.

9. The butterfly pieces are cut in pairs. These are glued back-to-back to reflect a double image.

10. Clean the mirror with vinegar and water. Apply dots of white glue with a toothpick to attach all the cutouts to the mirror. Gently clean away any excess glue with a cotton swab dipped in warm vinegar and water. Let dry.

11. Assemble the lamp.

12. Strips of eggshell paper can also be glued to the walnut cap plate and feet to trim the lamp. These should receive a few more coats of varnish for protection.

Horse Screen

■ The black and white screen (on page 109) forms a triptych of Japanese horse prints. Once again, eggshells are laboriously glued to rice paper. It should be noted that if this one aspect of orthodox decoupage is circumvented, eggshells can be glued directly to the screen. The outlines will not be as crisp, but the process will take far less time.

1. The 3-foot high screen is constructed of three masonite panels, sealed with shellac on back and front.

2. Up to ten coats of black oil base paint are applied to the panels, then sealed with one coat of varnish.

3. A fresh coat of varnish is applied and, while wet, gold leaf is sifted through a fine screen to speckle the surface. Once dry, this is sealed with two coats of spray varnish.

4. Twenty or more coats of varnish are added to finish the panels before any of the decoupage is affixed. Sand with #400-600 sandpapers every ten coats, then buff.

5. Eggshells are soaked in diluted liquid bleach for up to a week to clean and soften them. Dry thoroughly.

6. Three 12" x 14" sheets of heavy weight mulberry rice paper are painted with diluted black acrylic.

7. Unpainted eggshell fragments are glued into a tightly fitted pattern using tweezers. Wipe up excess glue with a damp cloth as you go. This is the most time-consuming phase of the project.

8. Once the sheets are complete, clean once more by gently wiping with a cloth dampened with warm water. Let dry.

9. Seal the paper with three coats of water base varnish.

10. Using patterns of prints enlarged on a photocopier, cut the horse shapes out of the eggshell paper.

11. Using a toothbrush, spatter indelible black ink over silver teapaper and let dry. Spray varnish to seal, then apply two more coats of varnish with a brush. This paper is used to outline the horse shapes.

12. When gluing the teapaper outlines and eggshell horse shapes to the screen, be very careful to glue them securely without allowing excess glue to ooze onto the screen. Let dry.

13. A few more coats of varnish will seal and bond the decoupage to the screen. Steel wool and wax.

14. The bamboo frame and fixtures can be spray painted or leafed with silver, then spattered with black ink. Seal with varnish, and install.

Butterfly Lamp

Horse Screen

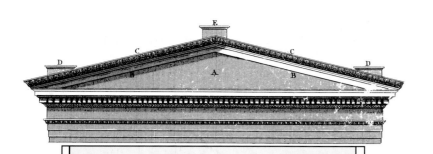

The images

that follow may be used to create your own projects. They may be suited to decorating particular objects you already have, or inspire you to find or make new objects. They can be photocopied to any scale and adapted for your own purposes. They can be left black and white, colored by hand, or photocopied onto unusual papers. Ultimately, they represent the mere beginning of a search for many more fascinating images you can use for decoupage.

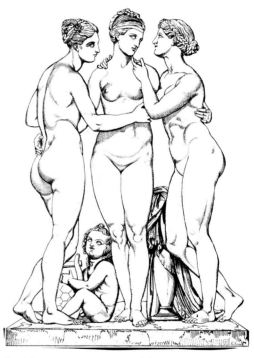

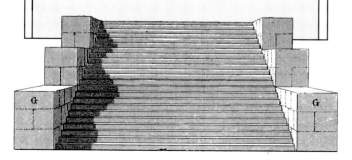

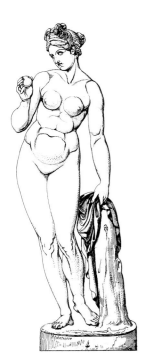

111

EN TOVT HONNEVR

REDOVBTE

112

113

32

14

Fig. 1

4

15

Fig. 30

Fig. 31

10

5

Fig. 3

34

Fig. 2

11

18

19

22

12

20

21

8

35

16

17

23

6

115

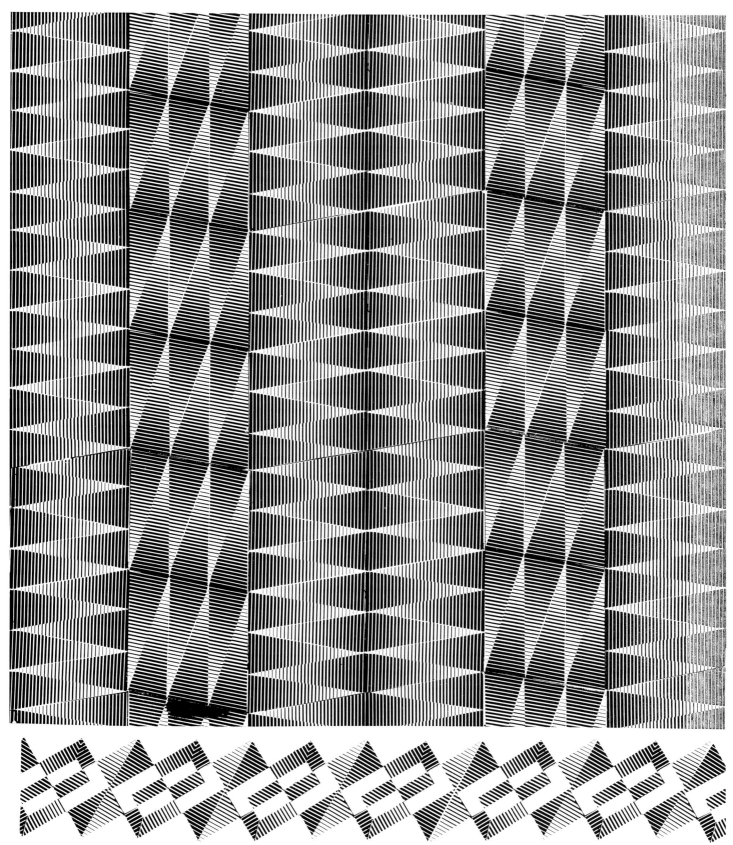

121

1   The Siskin

2   The Linnet

3   The Goldfinch

4   The Sparrow

5   The Bullfinch

6   The Mountain Sparrow

7   The Mountain Linnet

8   The Mountain Finch

Ea-gle	Fox	Grass-hop-per	Hunts-man
Inn	Kit-ten	Lamb	Mag-pie
Night-in-gale	Ox	Par-rot	Quiv-er
Rab-bit	Swan	Tur-key	Uni-corn
Whale	Xerx-es	Yel-low-ham-mer	Ze-bra

ABCDE
FGHIK
LMNOP
QRSTU
VWXYZ

▲

Acrylic: a paint or medium which is plastic-based, water-soluble while wet, but non-soluble and permanent when dry.

Collage: a design in which components may overlap and be of mixed media.

Decal: a precolored design on paper that can be transferred to a surface.

Eggshell inlay: a mosaic made with broken bits of eggshell, usually covered with many coats of varnish.

Gesso acrylic: can be used as a primer, sealer, filler, stiffener and painting ground for oils, acrylics or watercolors.

Glaze: a finishing coat, such as thinned and tinted varnish, used over a painted object for a softening effect.

Gloss medium: an acrylic polymer latex solution which can be used as an adhesive or a clear textured varnish.

Gold leaf: can be real gold or faux (also known as metal leaf, composition leaf or dutch metal) and applied as small, thin sheets.

Gold paper braid: embossed foil paper, often used in Victorian decoupage.

Gold size: the adhesive used to attach the leaf to an object, allowed to partially dry until sticky.

Mosaic: a design composed of small pieces of inlaid tile, glass, stone, wood, paper, etc.

Mother-of-pearl flakes: Iridescent bits from the inner layer of certain shells.

Oil pencils: commonly called "colored pencils," used to color prints.

Paper-mâché: paper strips mixed with glue, layered and pressed to form foundations for decoupage. A pulp variety known as "instant paper-mâché" can be used to fill the embossed cavities in respoussé.

Repoussé: embossing, molding and stuffing a decoupage print to create a raised relief.

Sealer: either alcohol-diluted shellac or acrylic spray used to protect a decoupage print or foundation object.

Shellac: diluted with alcohol and used to seal paper prints or raw wood foundations.

Solvent: used to dilute or clean a specific finish (e.g. turpentine for varnish, acetone for lacquer, water for acrylic).

Sticky tack: a putty used to hold a decoupage design temporarily in place.

Trompe l'oeil: an optical illusion giving a flat object the appearance of depth, meaning to "fool the eye."

Varnish: available in many variations, used to finish the entire piece of decoupage.

White glue: standard PVA or PVC glues, usually thinned with water for decoupage.

Credits

Projects and examples provided by:

Cynthia Alderdice: pages 14, 32, 33, 97

Nora Blose: 82, 83

Andy Buck: 53

Brigid Burns: 24, 25

Bob Clark & Holly Boswell: 36, 37

Elaine Covington: 34, 35 (with Joshua Goldberg), 50

Nancy Crage: 105

Polly Degas: 12, 81, 84, 85, 90, 91, 100, 104, 105

Ann Douglas: 15

Fred Gaylor: 34, 38–41, 43

Helen La Rose: 92, 93

Anne McCloskey: 44, 60, 61

Patricia Nimocks: 94

Beth Palmer: 51

Carol Perry: 28, 29, 62, 63, 66, 67, 74, 75, 81, 86, 87, 89, 101, 104

Tom Sullivan: 2, 6, 56, 57

Terry Taylor: 10, 95

Happy Veirs: 14, 28, 54, 64, 70, 71, 78, 79, 108, 109

Ellen Zahorec: 7, 11, 40, 42, 44–50, 52, 53, 55, 58, 59

Incidental instructional text provided by:

Cynthia Alderdice, Polly Degas, Carol Perry, and Happy Veirs

Special thanks to Patricia Nimocks and Polly Degas for their gracious assistance.

Index

A

acrylic ..18, 19, 22, 23, 31, 32
amber varnish 26
Antoinette, Marie 9
arte povero 8

B

baby bottle 26
bloom 18, 27
bole 65, 102
bubbles 27

C

carta metallica 68, 69, 72, 76, 99, 102
ceramics 12, 18, 19, 31
collage..10, 31, 51–54, 59–61
Contemporary decoupage ..8, 10
cracks 27, 103
Creil 30
cutting 22, 23, 80

E

eggshell 31, 105–107
18th century decoupage 8, 9, 16, 22
emboss 9, 30, 31, 88
epoxy 32, 102

F

foil 31, 73, 86, 99

furniture 8, 10, 13, 31

G

gesso 19, 31, 44, 57
glass 18,19, 23, 30–32, 73, 94
gold leaf 62, 63, 76, 77, 88, 99

I

inlay 30, 31

J

japanning 8

L

lacquer 8, 23, 26, 32
ladders 23
lithographs 16

M

moonstone 32
mother-of-pearl 31, 65, 72, 73, 76, 77

O

oil pencils 22, 27, 68, 80

P

pantyhose 27
paper-mâché 12, 31, 88
patina 26
photocopy 16, 31, 34, 36, 49, 51, 54, 59, 110

Pillement, Jean 9,63,80,102
polyurethane ...19, 32, 34, 39, 46, 47, 54
potichomania 30, 94, 98

R

repoussé 30, 88
rice paper 31, 35, 53, 54, 59, 77, 98, 99, 106, 107

S

shellac........18, 19, 22, 26, 32
silhouettes 23, 51, 102

T

toleware 30
trompe l'oeil 30

V

varnish drips 27
Victorian decoupage 8, 9
vinegar 22, 23, 103, 106

W

wood 12, 18, 31

X

X-acto knife 22,72,76,96,98

Y

Yatsuhashi 65, 76